How to preserve your psychological health

By

MAHMOUD

"How to preserve your psychological health without being influenced by the negative attitudes of others"

In this exercise you will learn how to:

Feel calmer

Relax before and during stressful situations

Face negative thoughts and replace them with positive ones.

CONTENTS

(1)

The psychological equation is:

Your ideas, thoughts, and beliefs influence your behavioural actions and bodily responses.

If your thoughts are negative, your behavioural actions and bodily responses will be negative;

Whereas if your thoughts are positive, your behavioural actions and bodily responses will be positive.

(2)

Look at the photos.

Here we will show you a few photos.

Notice your feelings, whatever they may be. Record them along with your ideas (Choose the method of recording – notes, video, or audio).

(3)

What is required to be done is:

Implement the following steps as part of the training:

1. Relax and breathe deeply, then exhale slowly (3 times).
2. Look at the photo and the negative expressions it bears.
3. Replace those expressions with positive ones (replace sad expressions with happy ones, depression with joy, anger with serenity, and such) while repeating in your mind "I am calm and relaxed; my mind is calm, and I feel inner tranquillity", while smiling.
4. Repeat this with each photo.
5. Overcome any various thoughts that deter you from performing this exercise.
6. After mastering this technique, document your positive state, along with the feelings and ideas that accompany you in this positive state (documenting may be by writing, taking a video of one's self, or taking a personal photo).
7. Send your documented positive state to the trainer for evaluation.

By being able to imagine yourself in your positive state and document it while repeating positive statements while smiling followed by the trainer's evaluation, you will attain the life that you deserve to live.

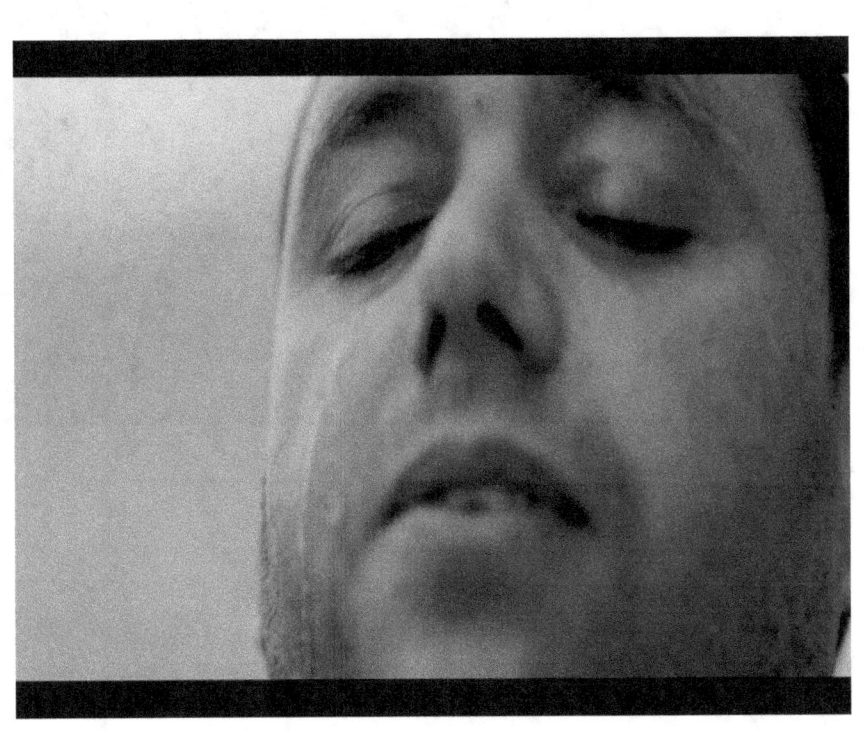

Implement the following steps as part of the training:

1. Relax and breathe deeply, then exhale slowly (3 times).
2. Look at the photo and the negative expressions it bears.
3. Replace those expressions with positive ones (replace sad expressions with happy ones, depression with joy, anger with serenity, and such) while repeating in your mind "I am calm and relaxed; my mind is calm, and I feel inner tranquillity", while smiling.
4. Repeat this with each photo.
5. Overcome any various thoughts that deter you from performing this exercise.
6. After mastering this technique, document your positive state, along with the feelings and ideas that accompany you in this positive state (documenting may be by writing, taking a video of one's self, or taking a personal photo).
7. Send your documented positive state to the trainer for evaluation.

By being able to imagine yourself in your positive state and document it while repeating positive statements while smiling followed by the trainer's evaluation, you will attain the life that you deserve to live.

<u>If you need any help, you may contact the trainer.</u>

Dr. Mahmoud

malmostshar@yahoo.com

info@ihossa.com